ONLY YOKING

TOP-DOWN KNITTING PATTERNS FOR 12 SEAMLESS YOKE SWEATERS

OLGA PUTANO

DAVID & CHARLES

www.davidandcharles.com

CONTENTS

INTRODUCTION

Growing up in Ukraine, my mother often made us our clothing. Sometimes it was from an old curtain that was getting no use, sometimes from scraps of fabric that came from my grandma, and rarely from a new piece of fabric – she knew how to create something amazing out of ordinary items. She knitted us little socks and sometimes a sweater. I remember being in awe of how she was able to take something like a strand of wool or a flat sheet of fabric and create something three-dimensional.

Once I was about six years old, I wanted to give it a try, too. My mom patiently taught me the crafts and I took off running. I made clothing for my doll and repeatedly asked my grandma for scraps of fabric and yarn, which she always gifted to me if she had them. I continued these two crafts (with others sprinkled in) on and off throughout my childhood and then into adulthood.

When I became a mother, I stuck to knitting more so than sewing, as I could do it anywhere, and it didn't take much effort or physical energy, which I was running short on in those days. One day, I had an idea pop up in my mind of a yoke sweater. When I couldn't find a pattern that resembled the image in my mind, I humbly and nervously decided to try to design it myself. That later became my first self-published knitting pattern, and I was hooked!

I hope this book gives you plenty of reasons to cast on yet another project, and I hope the sweaters keep you cozy. Let your handiwork be worn often, mended and be passed on through generations.

Enjoy!

Olga

HOW TO USE THIS BOOK

This book consists of 12 yoke sweaters in three different yarn weight sections – four sweaters in each section – from warmest to lightest fabrics. Once you spot the sweater you'd like to make first, follow the pattern for the yarn weight, which you will find at the end of the section, checking the size you should be working to by consulting the overview at the beginning of the section, and referring to the chart for knitting the yoke of the specific sweater you have chosen when directed.

WHY KNIT CIRCULAR YOKES?

I have designed and published a few different styles and constructions of sweaters. All have their own advantages. I consistently design top down, circular yoke sweaters because of how easy it is to make this garment fit to your unique body.

The top down construction allows you to try on the sweater as you knit, confirming that the yoke is long or short enough, ensuring the sleeves fit well and customizing the length of the body. There is absolutely no seaming involved, so once you bind / cast off those last stitches, other than weaving in ends and blocking, you're done!

Yoke sweaters are also great for beginner garment knitters – there are only a handful of techniques used in a basic pattern.

For the colorwork sweaters in this book, you'll need to know how to: cast on, bind / cast off, knit, purl, make a new stitch (leaning left and right), decrease stitches (k2tog and ssk) and cast on with the backwards loop method. That's it! If you're already comfortable with working cable stitches, you can move on to the textured designs in this book.

Yoke sweaters are a great place to start when you're new to garment knitting, and also a relaxing yet engaging project for a more advanced knitter.

STARTING YOUR PROJECT

When deciding on which sweater you'd like to make, first choose the yarn weight. Are you going to make a warm and cozy one that's also quicker to finish (a worsted / aran sweater pattern)? Are you going for something more intricate that takes a bit longer and lets you savor every stitch until you end up with a perfect layering garment (a fingering / 4ply sweater pattern)? Or maybe you'll go for something in the middle, and more versatile for a variety of seasons (a DK / double knitting sweater pattern).

Once you've made your choice, head to the chapter of this book corresponding with the yarn thickness you've chosen. Look over the four yokes in that section and decide on the one you'd like to make.

At the end of each chapter is the written pattern instructions for the full sweater in worsted / aran, DK / double knitting, or fingering / 4ply weight yarn. Follow the same pattern to work any of the yokes for that yarn thickness. When instructed in the pattern to "Work from chart", follow the chart for the specific yoke you've chosen. It's that simple!

KNITTING FROM THE TOP DOWN

Knitting a sweater from the top down begins with the neckband. After that comes a bit of stitch increasing and neck shaping to make the sweater fit nicely and cover the back of your neck.

Now you are ready for the fun part – the yoke! Once you've worked a chart and your yoke is long enough to fit specifically you, you can divide for sleeves and place those stitches on hold while you work on the body of the sweater.

When the body is finished, you will move on to the sleeves – putting the sleeve stitches back onto your needles, picking up a few for the underarm and working some decreases to shape a sleeve that fits well. Yoke sweaters are completely seamless and worked in the round.

TOOLS & MATERIALS

The joy of knitting is that with colorful yarn, your favorite needles and just a few other small items, you can work on your project anywhere. Here you will find information about all you will need to make a sweater from this book and how to choose your needles, yarn and notions.

NEEDLES

For these sweaters, you'll need circular needles in different lengths to hold the changing number of stitches throughout. Wherever the circumference is smaller (like the neckline and sleeves), you can work with a longer circular needle or use a set of DPNs (double pointed needles). The yoke increases add a lot of stitches, so switch to a longer circular needle to avoid the fabric bunching up.

I love using sharp stainless steel needles as the stitches glide smoothly over them, but if you're a new knitter, give wooden needles a try. Stitches stay in place and don't slide around on them too much, so you can more easily work on your technique.

When choosing your needles, remember that the size of them isn't what's important – getting gauge with them is (see Getting the Best Results).

The needle sizes here are a suggestion you can start with. Work a swatch in stockinette / stocking stitch in the round, block the swatch and check the gauge to decide if you need to go up or down a needle size.

For the worsted / aran weight sweaters: US 8 / 5mm main needle (or size needed to obtain gauge), US 6 / 4mm for ribbing (or two sizes smaller than the gauge needle).

For the DK / double knitting weight sweaters: US 6 / 4mm main needle (or size needed to obtain gauge), US 4 / 3.5mm for ribbing (or two sizes smaller than the gauge needle).

For the fingering / 4ply weight sweaters: US 4 / 3.5mm main needle (or size needed to obtain gauge), US 2 / 2.75mm for ribbing (or two sizes smaller than the gauge needle).

Knitting needles can be measured in various ways to indicate the width of the needle, and have different systems to mark the size.

The needle sizes table will help you make sure you have the correct size needle for your project, whether you use US, metric or UK standards.

Start with the recommended needle size when making your swatch, then adjust the size up or down if needed to achieve the same gauge as given in the overview at the beginning of the yarn weight section. Once you've picked your needle size to obtain gauge, move up the table by 2 rows to determine the needle size you should use for the ribbing.

Needle sizes

US	METRIC	UK
0	2mm	14
1	2.25mm	13
2	2.75mm	12
-	3mm	11
3	3.25mm	10
4	3.5mm	-
5	3.75mm	9
6	4mm	8
7	4.5mm	7
8	5mm	6
9	5.5mm	5
10	6mm	4
10.5	6.5mm	3
-	7mm	2
-	7.5mm	1
11	8mm	0

YARN

As you choose yarn for your project, think about how you are planning on wearing it. Do you live in a cold climate and like to layer your sweaters? You can go for a more rustic yarn or any wool in general. Do you want to wear your sweater close to your skin? Choose a yarn with some baby alpaca or baby yak. Looking for something to wear on chilly summer nights? Choose a wool blend with cotton or silk. And if you'd like to wear your knits in the sun, choose cotton, linen, silk or any combination of these.

Throughout the world, different names are often used for various yarn types and thicknesses. The yarn weights table, which lists yarn weights from thinnest to thickest, can help you navigate this as you search for the right yarn for your sweater.

Yarn weights

US	UK	OTHER NAMES
Lace	Lace, 2ply	Cobweb
Light fingering	3ply	Sock yarn, Baby yarn
Fingering	4ply, Sock yarn	Baby yarn, Super fine
Sport	5ply	Heavy fingering, Fine
DK	DK, Double knitting	Light worsted, 8ply, Light
Worsted	Aran	10ply, Medium

It is less important what a yarn is called, and more important whether you achieve the correct gauge called for in the pattern. Knit a swatch with your chosen yarn and check your gauge. If needed, try with different needle sizes until you can achieve the gauge given for the pattern.

You can also hold two strands of yarn together to act as a thicker gauge yarn. For example, holding two strands of a light fingering / 3ply weight yarn together may substitute for a DK / double knitting weight yarn. However, depending on the yarn properties, they may also match better to a worsted / aran weight gauge. This is why trying the yarn and measuring your gauge is so important before you begin.

NOTIONS

For all sweaters, you'll need a stitch marker to mark the beginning of the round; scrap yarn for holding the sleeve stitches - make sure this is a smooth fiber and thinner than the yarn you are knitting with; and a tapestry needle for weaving in ends. Of course you'll also need your measuring tape and a pair of small scissors.

For the textured yokes, you'll also need a cable needle to work the cable stitches. The cable needle should be the same size or smaller than your gauge needle so you do not stretch out the stitches.

The chart for Naomi includes a bobble and I prefer the half double crochet bobble. If you want to make bobbles in this way, you'll also need a crochet hook in the same size as your main needles.

For blocking, you'll need some wool wash for soaking your sweater, towels for squeezing out the water, and space to lay out your beautiful new sweater while you wait for it to dry.

FOLLOWING THE PATTERNS

The chapters for the three yarn weights - worsted / aran, DK / double knitting and fingering / 4ply weight yarn – each show four yoke options followed by the full sweater pattern for that yarn weight. Work through the pattern, and when instructed follow the chart for your chosen yoke option.

HOW TO READ A CHART

Once you learn how to read a chart, your knitting experience will likely be revolutionized. Not only is it easier than working from written instructions, you will gain confidence in knowing that you can knit from either kind of pattern. Colorwork patterns usually do not have written out chart instructions, too.

Working from a chart in the round versus flat has some differences, as well as working, say, brioche or mosaic from a chart. Here I explain how to read a chart for the given patterns – these are all working in the round. If you are unfamiliar with reading charts, I encourage you to read these instructions a couple of times before proceeding. It's really quite simple, but anything new can be a little challenging in the beginning.

Each square in a chart represents a stitch on the needles, or an action that you take. And now – the colors and symbols. What are those grey squares that disappear as the chart grows? Why, those are the "no stitch" squares! Confused? Don't be. You simply have to ignore the grey "no stitch" squares and continue to the next square that's in any other color. As you work your way through the chart, you will be making new stitches (whenever you see the "make one left / right" symbol) and the "no stitch" squares will lessen with every increase round. The key next to the chart will tell you which squares match which yarn color in the pattern, and you simply knit the stitch in the specified color. Whenever the chart has a symbol in a square you're about to work, look again at the chart key to see what kind of stitch (purl, cable, etc.) you are to work in the square with the appropriate color. Note that cabled stitches will take up more than one square, as the technique uses at least two stitches.

A chart made for yoke sweaters is repeated over and over again until all the stitches on your needles have been worked for a full round. To begin, you will always read the chart from right to left - every round begins this way. Starting at the very bottom right corner, you will begin the first round by working the first horizontal line of stitches from right to left. After you have knitted through the stitches on the chart, you are going to do it again – and again and again, until you arrive at the beginning of the next round on your needles. Then, you go on to the second round (second horizontal line of stitches) of the chart and continue this way until the chart has been completed.

CHART

cable motifs

grey boxes for
"no stitches"

round numbers

KEY

	knit
•	purl
	no stitch
	m1R
	m1L
	m1RP
	m1LP
	ssk
	k2tog
	1/1 LPC
	1/1 RPC
	1/1 LC
	1/1 RC
	2/1 RPC
	2/1 LPC
	2/1 RC
	2/1 LC
	2/2 RPC
	2/2 LPC
	2/2 LC
	2/2 RC

CHART

key showing MC, CC1, CC2

color to knit for next st

increase sts

KEY

	MC
	CC1
	CC2
	knit
	m1L
	no stitch

GETTING THE BEST RESULTS

Circular yoke sweaters are great projects because of how easy it is to make this type of garment fit to your body and preferences. However, you need to consider measurements and gauge first to get the right fit.

GAUGE & TENSION

Let's talk about gauge (also known as tension) – often seemingly a not-so-exciting part of knitting for many, but oh so important! So many knitters will admit to never making a swatch to obtain the correct gauge a pattern calls for. I used to be one of those knitters, too! But why is getting the correct gauge so important? When knitting a garment with the wrong gauge, your finished object will not fit correctly. Gauge too small – garment too small; gauge too large – your garment will be, too. Well, what if you're not making a garment, but a shawl or a scarf? Do you still need to spend the time on knitting, blocking and measuring a swatch? Absolutely! With the wrong gauge, the intended texture or drape of the finished knitted fabric will certainly differ, and you may end up unhappy with the outcome.

Yet another reason to spend the time on the swatch is that yarn requirements in any given pattern can change drastically if your gauge doesn't match what the pattern specifies.

Whatever gauge any given pattern calls for can sometimes be achieved through a different weight yarn. For example: for the DK / double knitting weight gauge used in this book, you may be able to use heavy fingering weight, sport weight or even light worsted weight yarn. If you can achieve the specified gauge with a different weight yarn than the pattern calls for AND you are happy with the drape and texture this yarn gives you – you can absolutely use it! So friends, let's learn to enjoy the slow process of making our garments, and let's make sure we actually want to wear them once they're finished. Take that little bit of time to knit your swatch, to make sure the rest of your time working on your project doesn't go to waste.

SIZING & EASE

How do you choose a size to make your sweater in? We all have varying tastes in how we like our sweaters to fit. I, myself, have various sizes of pullovers and cardigans in my cedar chest. The close fitting one to wear with my generous wide-legged bottoms, a slightly roomier one that pairs so well with my favorite pair of jeans, and even ridiculously oversized ones that are perfect for freezing days when I have no plans of leaving the house. I love them all! But how do you decide, within this book?

The sweaters in this book are written to fit with about 2-4 inches / 5-10 centimeters of positive ease – or, this amount larger than your full bust measurement. But of course, you can look at other sizes to see if you'd prefer a size with more or less ease. What is important to take into consideration, other than bust circumference, is the sleeve circumference. If you size down, will the sleeve circumference also work for your body? If you size up, are you okay with going for sleeves with a fuller look?

The neckband will also vary between sizes, so keep this in mind. One way to help avoid a too-wide neckline if you happen to go for a larger size than the pattern suggests for your bust size is casting on with a smaller size needle – just make sure it isn't too tight and can still easily fit over your head.

YOKE, BODY & SLEEVE LENGTH

Because these sweaters are worked from the top down, you can really personalize the lengths of the yoke, body and sleeves to your exact preference, trying the garment on as you work on it.

Before dividng for the sleeves, try on the sweater and continue in stockinette / stocking stitch using the main color until you have reached the correct yoke length.

For the body and sleeves, you can customize the length by knitting more or less in the stockinette / stocking stitch portion before the ribbing.

Remember that these changes will also affect the yarn quantity requirements for your project.

OVERVIEW

Worsted / aran weight sweaters are so perfect for keeping super cozy in the coldest months of the year. They knit up quickly and I love feeling the thick strand of yarn glide through my fingers. The four sweaters in this chapter are a great starting place if you'd like to dip your toes into sweater knitting – simple enough for a beginner yet still engaging for an experienced knitter.

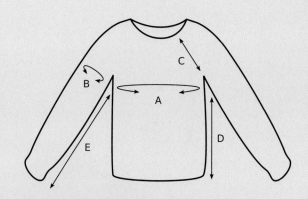

WHAT YOU WILL NEED:

NEEDLES

- US 8 / 5mm main needle (or size needed to obtain gauge)
- US 6 / 4mm for ribbing (or two sizes smaller than the gauge needle)

NOTIONS

- stitch marker
- scrap yarn
- tapestry needle
- cable needle (for Naomi and Daisie)
- crochet hook to match main needle size, optional (for Naomi bobbles)

CHOOSE YOUR SIZE:

FINISHED SIZES

SIZE	1	2	3	4	5	6	7	8	9	10
A: BUST CIRCUMFERENCE	32	36	40	44	48	52	56	60	64	68 in
	81.5	91.5	101.5	112	122	132	142	152.5	162.5	172.5 cm
B: UPPER SLEEVE CIRCUMFERENCE	12	13	14	16	17	18	20	21	22	23 in
	30.5	33	35.5	40.5	43	45.5	51	53.5	56	58.5 cm
C: YOKE LENGTH (AT FRONT)	8	8.5	9	9.5	10	10.25	10.5	10.75	11	11.25 in
	20.5	21.5	23	24	25.5	26	26.5	27.5	28	28.5 cm

D: BODY LENGTH (FROM UNDERARM TO HEM): 13in / 33cm

E: SLEEVE LENGTH (FROM UNDERARM TO CUFF): 17.5in / 44.5cm

GAUGE

16 sts x 20 rounds in stockinette / stocking stitch in the round, measured after blocking

Sienna   Daisie

Opal

SIENNA

Sienna offers an easy yoke to work, with a few rounds with longer floats and only a couple of rounds that use all three colors at the same time.

I loved working with this yarn as it gave the sweater a more rustic look with the yarn's halo effect.

Choose three colors that contrast well next to each other and get started. You'll be done in no time!

YARN YARDAGE / METERAGE

Yarn: The Fibre Co. Lore, 100% Kent lambswool, 100g 273 yards / 250 meters

SIZE	1	2	3	4	5	6	7	8	9	10
MC: "GENTLE"	734	790	846	903	959	1016	1072	1128	1185	1241 yd
	672	723	774	826	877	930	981	1032	1084	1135 m
CC1: "HEALER"	92	99	107	114	122	130	137	145	152	160 yd
	84	91	98	104	112	119	125	133	139	146 m
CC2: "HAPPINESS"	81	88	95	102	109	115	122	130	138	146 yd
	74	80	87	94	100	105	112	119	126	134 m

PATTERN NOTES

If you have a short torso like me, and like to layer your clothing, consider making a slightly shorter body. Alternatively, you may choose to make it a bit longer for the colder months and even work it into a tunic or dress! So many possibilities - just remember that these changes will affect how much yarn you use and plan accordingly.

SIENNA CHART

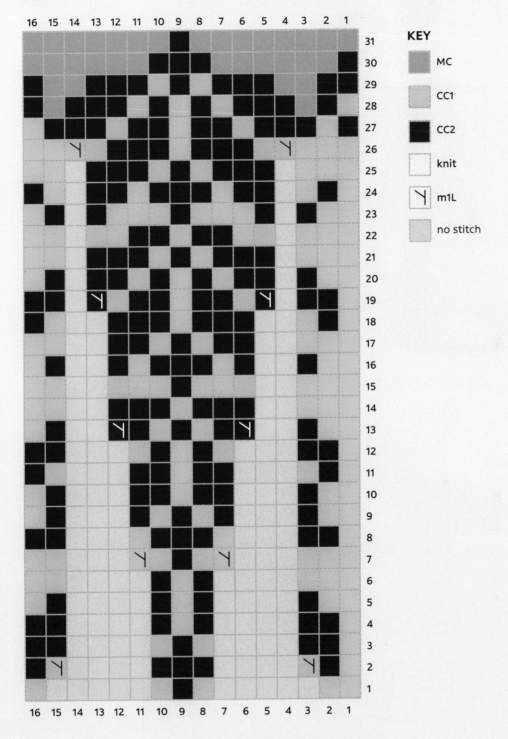

KEY

- MC
- CC1
- CC2
- knit
- m1L
- no stitch

OPAL

Opal is a great beginner colorwork sweater. Only two colors at a time are utilized throughout and only a few rounds have floats that are long enough to need catching.

Choose two colors that have good contrast between each other for the yoke and pick a third complementary color for the rest of the sweater.

Try out different combinations when swatching to experiment with the two contrast colors - starting with a dark color rather than a light one can create a very different effect for the yoke.

YARN YARDAGE / METERAGE

Yarn: Julie Asselin Journey Worsted, 80% merino / 20% Targhee wool, 115g 210 yards / 192 meters

SIZE	1	2	3	4	5	6	7	8	9	10
MC: "DENTELLES"	645	716	787	858	929	1000	1071	1142	1213	1284 yd
	590	655	720	785	850	915	979	1044	1109	1174 m
CC1: "AUTOMNE"	93	100	108	116	124	131	139	147	154	162 yd
	85	92	99	106	113	120	127	134	141	148 m
CC2: "MENTHE"	118	128	138	148	158	168	178	188	198	208 yd
	108	117	126	135	144	154	163	172	181	190 m

PATTERN NOTES

Choose two colors with very high contrast for CC1 and CC2, with a complementary color for MC. Solid colors and semi-solids are fun options for colorwork designs. I personally love lots of contrast to make the motif stand out. A speckled colorway in the background can also add a bit of sparkle to your project, but be careful not to use a color that's prevalent in the speckles as a contrast color.

OPAL CHART

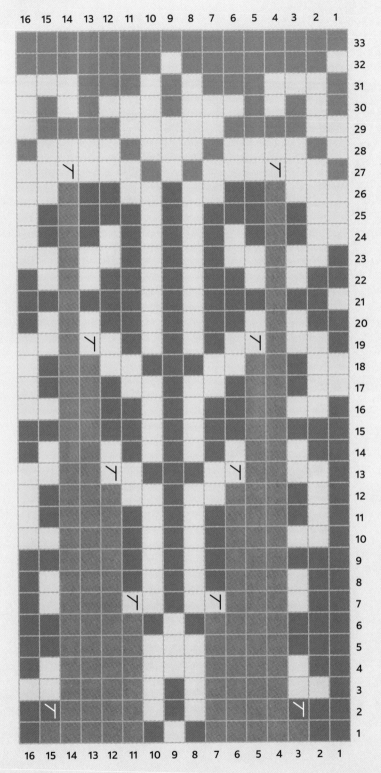

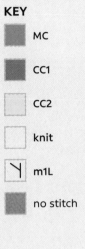

KEY

- MC
- CC1
- CC2
- knit
- m1L
- no stitch

NAOMI

Naomi utilizes cables, bobbles and simple knit and purl stitches to create lots of depth and texture.

There are many ways to create a bobble, so choose your favorite way, or if you are still on the hunt to find the one you love, I suggest trying my favorite – half double crochet bobble.

The yarn I used here is very smooth, which helped the stitches glide smoothly while creating all the fun twists and turns on this yoke.

YARN YARDAGE / METERAGE

Yarn: Woolberry Fiber Co. Berry Worsted, 100% superwash merino, 100g 218 yards / 199 meters

SIZE	1	2	3	4	5	6	7	8	9	10
MC: "MY FAVORITE SWEATER"	851	916	981	1047	1112	1178	1243	1308	1374	1439 yd
	778	838	897	958	1017	1077	1137	1196	1257	1316 m

PATTERN NOTES

The cable stitches use two, three and four stitches, as well as knit and purl stitches, so follow the instructions for each cable symbol carefully. Make sure to use the correct type of increase, with either a left or right direction as indicated in the chart, to maintain the pattern.

Another way to add even more depth and texture is choosing a speckled yarn for this project. Make some swatches in different yarns to help you decide on the look you're going for.

NAOMI CHART

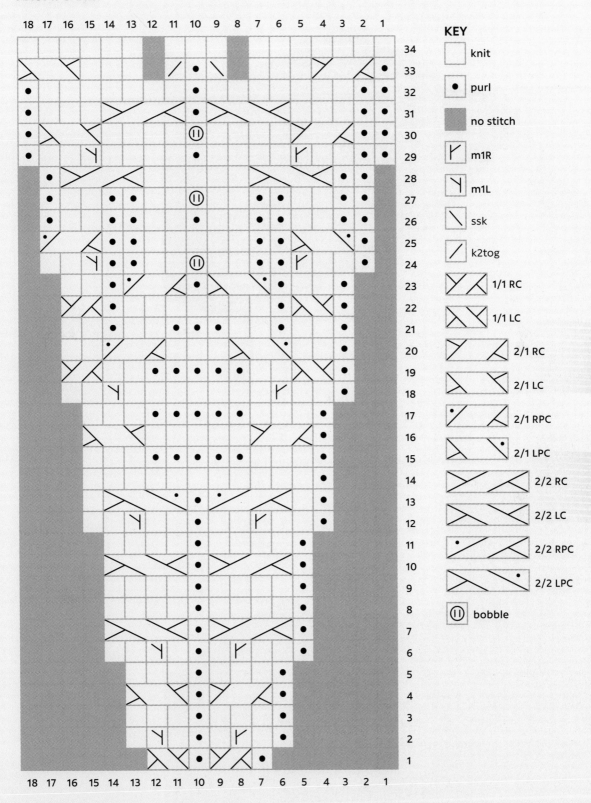

KEY

☐	knit
•	purl
▨	no stitch
⅄	m1R
⅄	m1L
⟍	ssk
⟋	k2tog
⤬	1/1 RC
⤬	1/1 LC
⤬	2/1 RC
⤬	2/1 LC
⤬	2/1 RPC
⤬	2/1 LPC
⤬	2/2 RC
⤬	2/2 LC
⤬	2/2 RPC
⤬	2/2 LPC
Ⓘ	bobble

DAISIE

For a lot of my patterns my inspiration comes from flowers and nature in general.

Daisie is a textured, cabled yoke sweater inspired by sunflower petals. The twists and turns dance through the yoke and finally meet to a soft point at the end.

This rustic yet soft yarn is really great at locking those cabled stitches in place. Choose a colorway that has great depth to make those textures pop.

YARN YARDAGE / METERAGE

Yarn: The Farmer's Daughter Fibers Pishkun, 100% Rambouillet wool, 100g 255 yards / 233 meters

SIZE	1	2	3	4	5	6	7	8	9	10
MC: "DIRTY LITTLE DANDELION"	832	898	960	1024	1088	1152	1216	1280	1344	1408 yd
	761	821	878	937	995	1054	1112	1171	1229	1288 m

PATTERN NOTES

The cable stitches use two, three and four stitches, as well as knit and purl stitches, so follow the instructions for each cable symbol carefully. Make sure to use the correct type of increase, with either a left or right direction and in knit or purl as indicated in the chart, to maintain the pattern and help strongly define the cable motifs.

Worsted / aran weight sweaters are worn in cold weather. If your sweaters ride down the back of your neck, that can't be very cozy. To help remedy this issue, you can work a couple more rows of short row neck shaping. This will make the back neck of the sweater just a bit higher up, so you can be covered up in the chilly winter.

DAISIE CHART

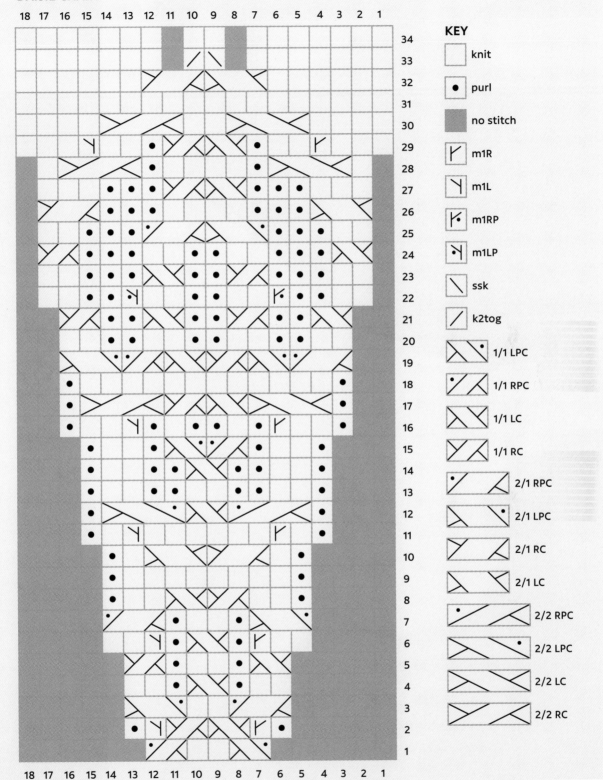

KEY

☐	knit
•	purl
▨	no stitch
Ⲡ	m1R
Ⲥ	m1L
Ⲡ•	m1RP
•Ⲥ	m1LP
╲	ssk
╱	k2tog
╲•	1/1 LPC
•╱	1/1 RPC
╲╲	1/1 LC
╲╱	1/1 RC
•╲╲	2/1 RPC
╲╲•	2/1 LPC
╲╲	2/1 RC
╱╱	2/1 LC
•╲╲	2/2 RPC
╲╲•	2/2 LPC
╲╲	2/2 LC
╲╱	2/2 RC

WORSTED / ARAN SWEATER PATTERN

Knitting with worsted / aran weight yarn is one of my favorite hobbies in the colder months. Wearing the garment I make with this yarn is a close second. It is just so warm and cozy!

You can choose soft colors and rustic yarn to bring a halo over your sweater, or use colors with lots of contrast in a high-ply tightly spun fiber, which offers a crisp stitch definition.

If you are a knitter that cannot wait to wear your project and you love spending time outdoors in chilly weather, or you just love to be bundled up, pick a good plump yarn, let it glide over your fingers and in no time you'll have a garment that will keep you warm for years to come.

PATTERN

Using smaller gauge needles and Sienna CC2 / Opal CC2 / Naomi MC / Daisie MC, loosely cast on (62,64,68) 72,74,76 (76,80,84) 88 sts using long tail or your preferred method. PM for back of neck and join to work in the round. This will be your BOR.

R1: *k1, p1* rep to BOR.

Repeat R1 three more times.

Switch to main gauge needles.

Change to Sienna CC1 / Opal CC1 or continue with Naomi MC / Daisie MC.

INC. ROUND

Size 1: *(k4, m1L) three times, k3, m1L* rep to last 2 sts, k2.

Size 2: *(k3, m1L) three times, k4, m1L* rep to last 12 sts, *k3, m1L* rep three more times.

Size 3: *k4, m1L, (k3, m1L) ten times* rep one more time.

Size 4: *k3, m1L* rep to BOR.

Size 5: *(k3, m1L) two times, k2, m1L* rep to last 2 sts, k2, m1L.

Size 6: *(k2, m1L) two times, k3, m1L* rep to last 6 sts, *k3, m1L* rep one more time.

Sizes 7-10: *k2, m1L* rep to BOR.

(78,84,90) 96,102,108 (114,120,126) 132 sts

SHORT ROW NECK SHAPING

I suggest using the German short row method, as it is the least visible one, in my opinion. You are welcome to use your favorite short row technique, where the instructions read "turn".

R1 (right side): k (19,21,23) 25,27,29 (31,33,35) 37, turn.

R2 (wrong side): purl back to BOR, sm, p (19,21,23) 25,27,29 (31,33,35) 37, turn.

R3 (right side): knit to 3 sts past the last turned st, turn.

R4 (wrong side): purl to 3 sts past the last turned st, turn.

Repeat R3 and R4 two more times. Knit to BOR.

Knit one round, resolving turned sts as you come to them (pick up the loop you previously wrapped around a stitch to turn for a short row, and knit it together with said stitch).

Work chart.

(208,224,240) 256,272,288 (304,320,336) 352 sts

Continue with MC in stockinette / stocking stitch, until work measures (8,8.5,9) 9.5,10,10.25 (10.5,10.75,11) 11.25 in / (20.5,21.5,23) 24,25.5,26 (26.5,27.5,28) 28.5 cm when measured at the front of the yoke. This is a good time to try on your yoke to make sure it fits your personal style. If needed, you can add more length before separating for sleeves - just remember that this will add a bit more yarn than specified in the yardage / meterage requirements.

From BOR, k (30,33,36) 38,41,44 (46,49,52) 55 sts.

Place the following (44,46,48) 52,54,56 (60,62,64) 66 sts on scrap yarn, for right sleeve.

Using the backwards loop method, cast on (4,6,8) 12,14,16 (20,22,24) 26 sts.

Knit the following (60,66,72) 76,82,88 (92,98,104) 110 sts.

Place the following (44,46,48) 52,54,56 (60,62,64) 66 sts on scrap yarn, for left sleeve.

Using the backwards loop method, cast on (4,6,8) 12,14,16 (20,22,24) 26 sts, placing a marker in the middle of these sts, for BOR.

(128,144,160) 176,192,208 (224,240,256) 272 sts

Continue in stockinette / stocking stitch in the round until body measures 11in / 28cm when measured from the cast on underarm sts, or until the body is 2in / 5cm shorter than your total preferred length.

HEM

Switch to smaller gauge needles.

R1: *k1, p1* rep to BOR.

Repeat R1 until hem measures 2in / 5cm.

Bind / cast off loosely, in pattern.

SLEEVES

Both sleeves are worked the same way.

Move one set of (44,46,48) 52,54,56 (60,62,64) 66 sleeve sts onto needles. Starting where the sts end and underarm begins, using MC, pick up and knit (4,6,8) 12,14,16 (20,22,24) 26 sts, plus one stitch on each side in the gap where the sleeve sts meet the underarm sts. PM in the middle of these underarm sts. This will be the BOR.

(50,54,58) 66,70,74 (82,86,90) 94 sts

R1: Knit until 1 st of the sleeve sts remains (before picked up sts), ssk, knit to BOR.

R2: Knit to the last picked up st (before sleeve sts), k2tog, knit to BOR.

(48,52,56) 64,68,72 (80,84,88) 92 sts

SLEEVE DECREASES

Step 1: knit (9,9,8) 7,5,4 (4,4,3) 3 rounds.

Step 2: k2, k2tog, knit to last 4 sts, ssk, k2.

Repeat Steps 1 and 2 (5,4,6) 7,9,11 (12,14,16) 15 more times.

(36,42,42) 48,48,48 (54,54,54) 60 sts

Then continue in stockinette / stocking stitch until sleeve measures 15in / 38cm when measured from the cast on underarm sts, or until the sleeve is 2in / 5cm shorter than your total preferred length.

DEC. ROUND

R1: *k4, k2tog* rep to BOR.

(30,35,35) 40,40,40 (45,45,45) 50 sts

Knit one round.

CUFF

Switch to smaller gauge needles.

Sizes 1,4,5,6,10: *k1, p1* rep to BOR.

Sizes 2,3,7,8,9: k2tog, p1, *k1, p1* rep to BOR.

(--,34,34) --,--,-- (44,44,44) -- sts

Continue in 1×1 rib until cuff measures 2in / 5cm.

Bind / cast off loosely, in pattern.

Repeat for second sleeve.

FINISHING

When you are done knitting your sweater, you'll need to do some finishing work to ensure lasting and professional looking results.

First you'll need to weave in all the yarn ends poking out where you began and ended sections of the sweater. Use a tapestry needle to weave in the ends loosely on the wrong side of the work, then carefully snip off the remaining yarn.

And last but not least, block your project. Soak your completed sweater in room temperature water and a little bit of wool wash, for 15-20 minutes. Next, pull it out of the water and squeeze it out. If you are using a yarn of animal fibers, you have to be careful here - gently squeeze the knitted fabric and do not agitate it as this risks felting the fabric. I will often lay the sweater between two towels, roll it up and gently walk on the rolled up towels. Now you'll want to lay the sweater out and shape it, to dry. It will dry in whatever form you leave it in, so make sure you shape it to the measurement specifications for your size.

Once your sweater is dry, you can wear it! Enjoy your hard work and stay cozy!

SIMPLY
VERSATILE
SWEATERS

OVERVIEW

DK / double knitting yarn is my favorite to design and knit with. It is the perfect in-between thickness that allows me to fit some special details into the design, and the final sweater is also a versatile piece in your wardrobe as well. The four sweaters in this chaper are really adaptable for a variety of yarns, just make sure to swatch and try out different sizes of needles to get the correct gauge and start knitting.

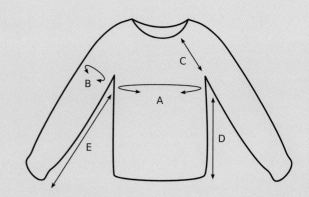

WHAT YOU WILL NEED:

NEEDLES

- US 6 / 4mm main needle (or size needed to obtain gauge)
- US 4 / 3.5mm for ribbing (or two sizes smaller than the gauge needle)

NOTIONS

- stitch marker
- scrap yarn
- tapestry needle
- cable needle (for Jana)

CHOOSE YOUR SIZE:

FINISHED SIZES

SIZE	1	2	3	4	5	6	7	8	9	10
A: BUST CIRCUMFERENCE	32	36	40	44	48	52	56	60	64	68 in
	81.5	91.5	101.5	112	122	132	142	152.5	162.5	172.5 cm
B: UPPER SLEEVE CIRCUMFERENCE	11.25	12.25	13.25	15	16	17	18.75	20.5	22.5	24.25 in
	28.5	31	33.5	38	40.5	43	47.5	52	57	61.5 cm
C: YOKE LENGTH (AT FRONT)	8	8.5	9	9.5	10	10.25	10.5	10.75	11	11.25 in
	20.5	21.5	23	24	25.5	26	26.5	27.5	28	28.5 cm

D: BODY LENGTH (FROM UNDERARM TO HEM): 13in / 33cm

E: SLEEVE LENGTH (FROM UNDERARM TO CUFF): 17.5in / 44.5cm

GAUGE

20 sts x 26 rounds in stockinette / stocking stitch in the round, measured after blocking

Masha

Jana

Audrie

MASHA

For Masha, choose two colors that have great contrast between each other, to use in the yoke section. Then add a third complementary color for the rest of the sweater. The yarn used in this sweater has excellent stitch definition which helps the colors pop against each other even more.

I made this sweater with a slightly cropped body. Remember that you can customize the length of your sweater by knitting more or less in the stockinette / stocking stitch portion of the body. Just remember that this will change the yarn quantity requirements for your project.

YARN YARDAGE / METERAGE

Yarn: Brooklyn Tweed Arbor Yarn, 100% American Targhee wool, 50g 145 yards / 133 meters

SIZE	1	2	3	4	5	6	7	8	9	10
MC: "MESA"	819	887	956	1024	1091	1160	1229	1297	1364	1431 yd
	749	811	874	937	998	1061	1124	1186	1248	1309 m
CC1: "DORADO"	192	208	224	240	256	272	287	303	319	335 yd
	176	190	205	220	234	249	262	277	292	306 m
CC2: "KLIMT"	189	205	221	236	252	268	283	299	315	331 yd
	173	187	202	216	230	245	259	273	288	303 m

PATTERN NOTES

Choose two colors with very high contrast for CC1 and CC2. Then select a complementary color for MC for the rest of the sweater. A springy yarn that has excellent stitch definition will help the chart design stand out and look crisp.

MASHA CHART

KEY

MC	(light gray)
CC1	(black)
CC2	(medium gray)
knit	(white)
m1L	(Y symbol)
no stitch	(gray)

JOSIE

For Josie, choose two colors with great contrast for the yoke section and pick a third complementary color for the rest of the project.

Before deciding on the yarn, try to picture how you'll wear the sweater. Do you like to layer under your sweaters? If so, you can go for a more rustic yarn. Soft fiber like the yarn I used here allows for the garment to be worn next to skin without irritation.

YARN YARDAGE / METERAGE

Yarn: mYak Baby Yak Medium, 100% baby yak, 50g 125 yards / 114 meters

SIZE	1	2	3	4	5	6	7	8	9	10
MC: "MUSTARD"	685	742	799	856	914	971	1028	1085	1142	1199 yd
	626	678	731	783	836	888	940	992	1044	1096 m
CC1: "DUSTY PINK"	190	206	222	238	253	269	285	301	317	333 yd
	174	188	203	218	231	246	260	275	290	305 m
CC2: "PETROL"	101	112	123	134	145	156	167	178	189	200 yd
	92	102	112	123	133	143	153	163	173	183 m

PATTERN NOTES

Choose two colors with very high contrast for CC1 and CC2. Then select a complementary color for MC for the rest of the sweater. In areas of the chart where there are longer distances between color changes, give an extra twist to the yarn to avoid long, loose floats.

JOSIE CHART

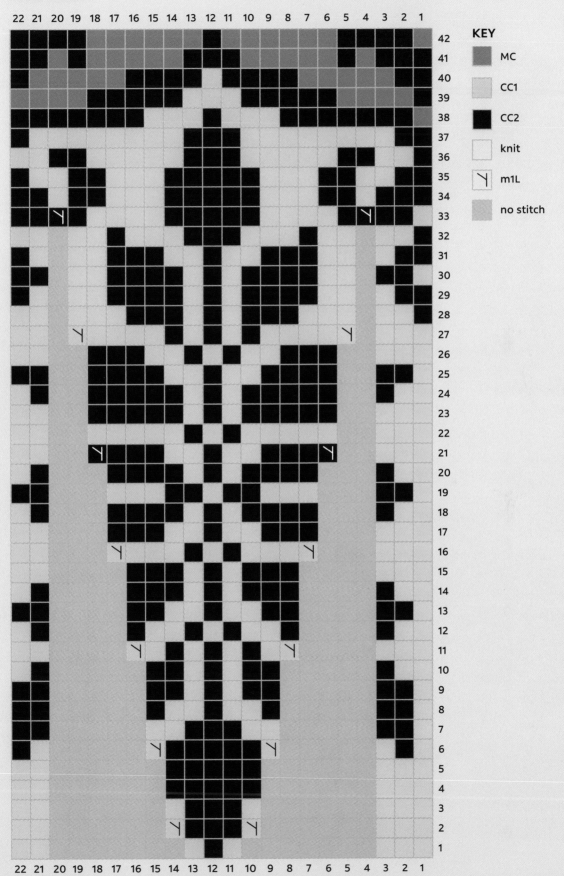

KEY

- MC
- CC1
- CC2
- knit
- ⅄ m1L
- no stitch

JANA

Jana is full of texture and a perfect opportunity to surround yourself with your favourite yarn color.

For this sweater, I used a fiber that has a bit of the rustic look yet a softer feel to it.

A yarn with a tighter twist and good stitch definition works great for cable motifs, if you want the design to pop. Knit a swatch with your yarn in pattern and see how you like it.

YARN YARDAGE / METERAGE

Yarn: Primrose Yarn Co. Roan DK, 60% American superwash merino / 40% domestic non superwash merino, 100g 230 yards / 210 meters

SIZE	1	2	3	4	5	6	7	8	9	10
MC: "TWILIGHT"	848	913	978	1044	1109	1174	1239	1305	1370	1435 yd
	776	835	895	955	1014	1074	1133	1193	1253	1313 m

PATTERN NOTES

The cable stitches use two, three and four stitches, as well as knit and purl stitches, so follow the instructions for each cable symbol carefully. Make sure to use the correct type of increase, with either a left or right direction and in knit or purl as indicated in the chart, to maintain the pattern and help strongly define the cable motifs.

JANA CHART

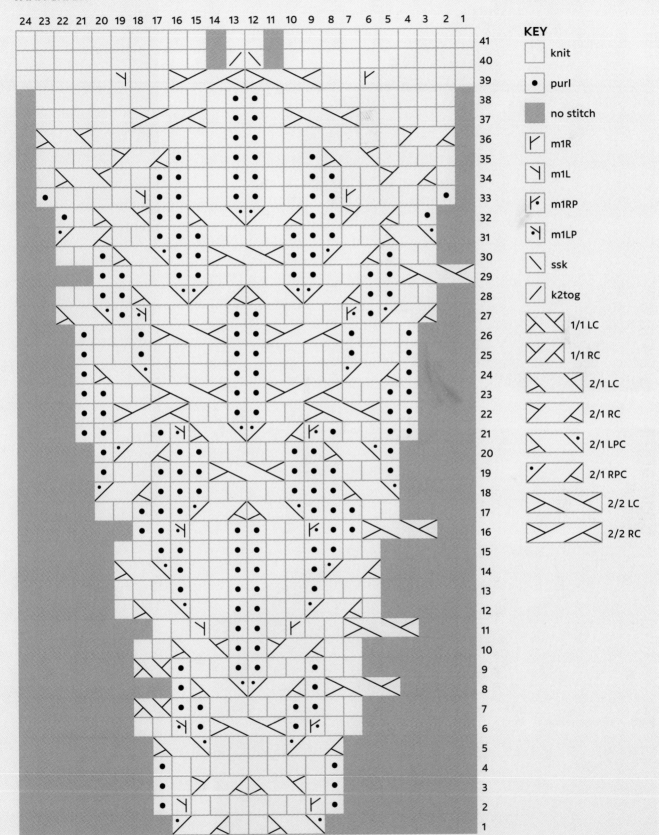

KEY

☐	knit
•	purl
▨	no stitch
⊢	m1R
⊣	m1L
⊬	m1RP
⊮	m1LP
\	ssk
/	k2tog
⟋⟍	1/1 LC
⟍⟋	1/1 RC
⟋ ⟍	2/1 LC
⟍ ⟋	2/1 RC
⟋ ⟍	2/1 LPC
⟍ ⟋	2/1 RPC
⟋⟍	2/2 LC
⟍⟋	2/2 RC

AUDRIE

For Audrie, you only need two colors, but of course you can play around and add more if you'd like – for example, switching the contrast color halfway through the yoke, or knitting the yoke in two colors and the body in a third. I recommend picking colors that have great contrast for colorwork, but explore different color combinations to discover what your style is.

Consider treating yourself to a luxury fiber like the one used here, and make a handmade heirloom garment that, if taken care of, will last.

YARN YARDAGE / METERAGE

Yarn: Clinton Hill Cashmere Company Bespoke DK Cashmere, 100% cashmere, 50g 125 yards / 114 meters

SIZE	1	2	3	4	5	6	7	8	9	10
MC: "PALE BLUSH"	600	675	750	825	900	975	1050	1125	1200	1275 yd
	549	617	686	754	823	891	960	1029	1097	1166 m
CC1: "TROPICAL TEAL"	107	116	125	134	143	152	161	170	180	189 yd
	98	106	114	123	131	139	147	155	165	173 m

PATTERN NOTES

Choose two colors with very high contrast for MC and CC1.
Be sure to fasten any floats that are longer than about
6 stitches. This will help keep your gauge consistent and
make it easier to put the sweater on without catching a
float with your finger. I usually follow an inch rule – if the
float is longer than 1in / 2.5cm, I catch it.

AUDRIE CHART

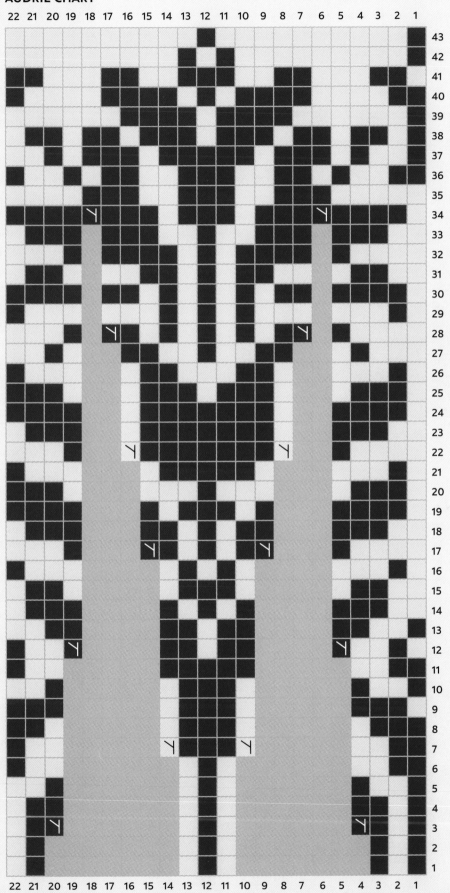

KEY

▧	MC
■	CC1
□	knit
⅄	m1L
▒	no stitch

DK / DOUBLE KNITTING SWEATER PATTERN

DK / double knitting weight yarn knits up fairly quickly, but still slow enough for you to enjoy the process.

Remember that you don't absolutely have to use DK weight yarn for the sweaters in this chapter. If you have a worsted / aran weight yarn you'd like to use, grab a needle size smaller than suggested in the pattern and knit a swatch. Play around with needle sizes until you get gauge the pattern calls for. Do you like the fabric this yarn has created? If so, go for it! And the opposite goes for a sport / 5ply weight yarn – go up a needle size until you acquire the correct gauge and make the decision on using the yarn based on the fabric it creates in said gauge. Explore the possibilities!

PATTERN

Using smaller gauge needles and Masha CC2 / Josie CC1 / Jana MC / Audrie MC, loosely cast on (84,90,90) 90,96,102 (104,108,112) 112 sts using long tail or your preferred method. PM for back of neck and join to work in the round. This will be your BOR.

R1: *k1, p1* rep to BOR.

Repeat R1 three more times.

Switch to main gauge needles.

Change to Masha CC1 or continue with Josie CC1 / Jana MC / Audrie MC.

INC. ROUND

Size 1: *k7, m1L* rep to BOR.

Size 2: k6, m1L, k6, m1L, *k7, m1L, k6, m1L* rep to BOR.

Size 3: *k4, m1L* rep to last 2 sts, k2.

Sizes 4-6: *k3, m1L* rep to BOR.

Size 7: k4, m1L, k3, m1L, *k2, m1L, k3, m1L* rep to last 7 sts, k4, m1L, k3, m1L.

Size 8: k2, m1L, k2, m1L, *k2, m1L, k3, m1L* rep to last 4 sts, k2, m1L, k2, m1L.

Size 9: *k2, m1L, k2, m1L, k3, m1L* rep to BOR.

Size 10: *k2, m1L* rep to BOR.

(96,104,112) 120,128,136 (144,152,160) 168 sts

SHORT ROW NECK SHAPING

I suggest using the German short row method, as it is the least visible one, in my opinion. You are welcome to use your favorite short row technique, where the instructions read "turn".

R1 (right side): k (20,22,24) 27,30,33 (36,39,42) 44, turn.

R2 (wrong side): purl back to BOR, sm, p (20,22,24) 27,30,33 (36,39,42) 44, turn.

R3 (right side): knit to 4 sts past the last turned st, turn.

R4 (wrong side): purl to 4 sts past the last turned st, turn.

Repeat R3 and R4 two more times. Knit to BOR.

Knit one round, resolving turned sts as you come to them (pick up the loop you previously wrapped around a stitch to turn for a short row, and knit it together with said stitch).

Work chart.

(264,286,308) 330,352,374 (396,418,440) 462 sts

Continue with MC in stockinette / stocking stitch, until work measures (8,8.5,9) 9.5,10,10.25 (10.5,10.75,11) 11.25 in / (20.5,21.5,23) 24,25.5,26 (26.5,27.5,28) 28.5 cm when measured at the front of the yoke. This is a good time to try on your yoke to make sure it fits your personal style. If needed, you can add more length before separating for sleeves - just remember that this will add a bit more yarn than specified in the yardage / meterage requirements.

From BOR, k (39,43,47) 50,54,58 (61,64,67) 70 sts.

Place the following (54,57,60) 65,68,71 (76,81,86) 91 sts on scrap yarn, for right sleeve.

Using the backwards loop method, cast on (2,4,6) 10,12,14 (18,22,26) 30 sts.

Knit the following (78,86,94) 100,108,116 (122,128,134) 140 sts.

Place the following (54,57,60) 65,68,71 (76,81,86) 91 sts on scrap yarn, for left sleeve.

Using the backwards loop method, cast on (2,4,6) 10,12,14 (18,22,26) 30 sts, placing a marker in the middle of these sts, for BOR.

(160,180,200) 220,240,260 (280,300,320) 340 sts

Continue in stockinette / stocking stitch in the round until body measures 11in / 28cm when measured from the cast on underarm sts, or until the body is 2in / 5cm shorter than your total preferred length.

HEM

Switch to smaller gauge needles.

R1: *k1, p1* rep to BOR.

Repeat R1 until hem measures 2in / 5cm.

Bind / cast off loosely, in pattern.

SLEEVES

Both sleeves are worked the same way.

Move one set of (54,57,60) 65,68,71 (76,81,86) 91 sleeve sts onto needles. Starting where the sts end and underarm begins, using MC, pick up and knit (2,4,6) 10,12,14 (18,22,26) 30 sts, plus one stitch on each side in the gap where the sleeve sts meet the underarm sts. PM in the middle of these underarm sts. This will be the BOR.

(58,63,68) 77,82,87 (96,105,114) 123 sts

R1: Knit until 1 st of the sleeve sts remains (before picked up sts), ssk, knit to BOR.

R2: Knit to the last picked up st (before sleeve sts), k2tog, knit to BOR.

(56,61,66) 75,80,85 (94,103,112) 121 sts

SLEEVE DECREASES

Step 1: knit (10,10,10) 10,8,8 (5,4,3) 3 rounds.

Step 2: k2, k2tog, knit to last 4 sts, ssk, k2.

Repeat Steps 1 and 2 (3,3,5) 7,9,9 (13,15,19) 21 more times. (48,53,54) 59,60,65 (66,71,72) 77 sts

Then continue in stockinette / stocking stitch until sleeve measures 15in / 38cm when measured from the cast on underarm sts, or until the sleeve is 2.5in / 6.5cm shorter than your total preferred length.

DEC. ROUND

Sizes 1,3,5,7,9: *k4, k2tog* rep to BOR.

Sizes 2,4,6,8,10: k3, k2tog, *k4, k2tog* rep to BOR. (40,44,45) 49,50,54 (55,59,60) 64 sts

Knit one round.

CUFF

Switch to smaller gauge needles.

Sizes 1,2,5,6,9,10: *k1, p1* rep to BOR.

Sizes 3,4,7,8: k2tog, p1, *k1, p1* rep to BOR.

(--,--,44) 48,--,-- (54,58,--) -- sts

Continue in 1x1 rib until cuff measures 2in / 5cm.

Bind / cast off loosely, in pattern.

Repeat for second sleeve.

FINISHING

When you are done knitting your sweater, you'll need to do some finishing work to ensure lasting and professional looking results.

First you'll need to weave in all the yarn ends poking out where you began and ended sections of the sweater. Use a tapestry needle to weave in the ends loosely on the wrong side of the work, then carefully snip off the remaining yarn.

And last but not least, block your project. Soak your completed sweater in room temperature water and a little bit of wool wash, for 15-20 minutes. Next, pull it out of the water and squeeze it out. If you are using a yarn of animal fibers, you have to be careful here - gently squeeze the knitted fabric and do not agitate it as this risks felting the fabric. I will often lay the sweater between two towels, roll it up and gently walk on the rolled up towels. Now you'll want to lay the sweater out and shape it, to dry. It will dry in whatever form you leave it in, so make sure you shape it to the measurement specifications for your size.

Once your sweater is dry, you can wear it! Enjoy your hard work and stay cozy!

OVERVIEW

Fingering / 4ply weight sweaters are a perfectly light yet warming garment that can be worn in almost any season – light enough for a chilly summer evening, easy to layer in the colder months, and even perfect on its own in between! For me, designing and knitting with this thickness means I can fit intricate motifs into a small space. Take your time with your project and appreciate the details – give these patterns a try!

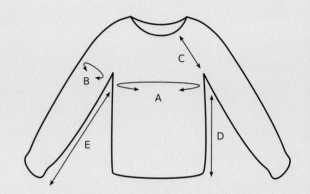

WHAT YOU WILL NEED:

NEEDLES

- US 4 / 3.5mm main needle (or size needed to obtain gauge)
- US 2 / 2.75mm for ribbing (or two sizes smaller than the gauge needle)

NOTIONS

- stitch marker
- scrap yarn
- tapestry needle
- cable needle (for Adeline)

CHOOSE YOUR SIZE:

FINISHED SIZES

SIZE	1	2	3	4	5	6	7	8	9	10
A: BUST CIRCUMFERENCE	32	36	40	44	48	52	56	60	64	68 in
	81.5	91.5	101.5	112	122	132	142	152.5	162.5	172.5 cm
B: UPPER SLEEVE CIRCUMFERENCE	12.5	13.5	15	15.75	16.5	17.5	19	20.5	22	23.5 in
	32	34.5	38	40	42	44.5	48.5	52	56	59.5 cm
C: YOKE LENGTH (AT FRONT)	8	8.5	9	9.5	10	10.25	10.5	10.75	11	11.25 in
	20.5	21.5	23	24	25.5	26	26.5	27.5	28	28.5 cm

D: BODY LENGTH (FROM UNDERARM TO HEM): 13in / 33cm

E: SLEEVE LENGTH (FROM UNDERARM TO CUFF): 17.5in / 44.5cm

GAUGE

24 sts x 28 rounds in stockinette / stocking stitch in the round, measured after blocking

Janey   Adeline

y

Mila

JANEY

Janey uses two contrasting colors to create a garment with a stunning yoke.

While choosing yarn for your colorwork project, take a photo of the two colors together and view it in black and white mode on your phone/camera. If the colors don't look very different, keep looking at different combinations. Once you see a big difference in the black and white photo, you're ready for a colorwork project that will show off the motif with strong contrast!

YARN YARDAGE / METERAGE

Yarn: Tot Le Matin Yarns Tot Single Mohair, 56% superwash merino / 44% mohair, 100g 437 yards / 400 meters

SIZE	1	2	3	4	5	6	7	8	9	10
MC: "COMORES"	1064	1136	1207	1278	1349	1420	1491	1562	1634	1706 yd
	973	1039	1104	1169	1234	1299	1364	1428	1494	1560 m
CC1: "CORETTE"	113	131	149	167	185	203	221	239	257	275 yd
	103	120	136	153	169	186	202	219	235	252 m

PATTERN NOTES

Choose two colors with very high contrast for MC and CC1. Be sure to fasten any floats that are longer than about 6 stitches. This will help keep your gauge consistent and make it easier to put the sweater on without catching a float with your finger. I usually follow an inch rule – if the float is longer than 1in / 2.5cm, I catch it.

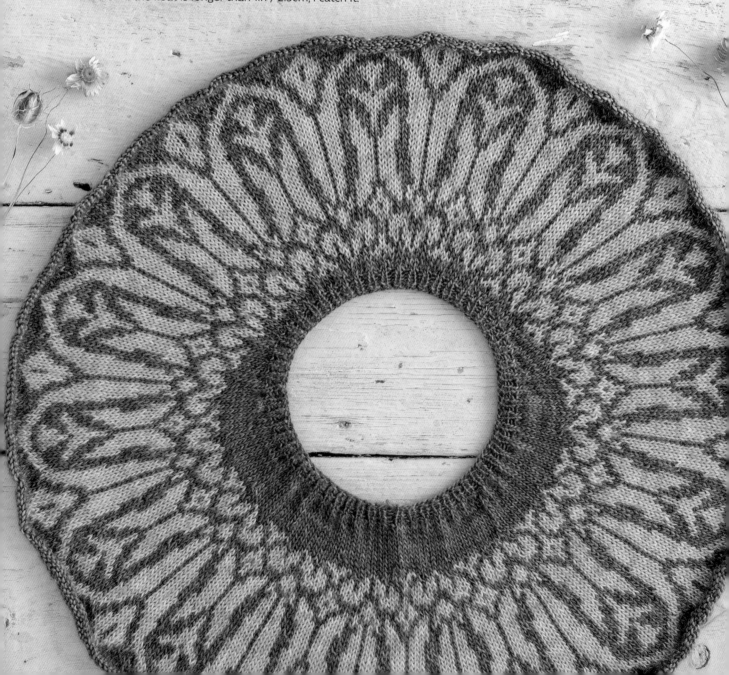

JANEY CHART

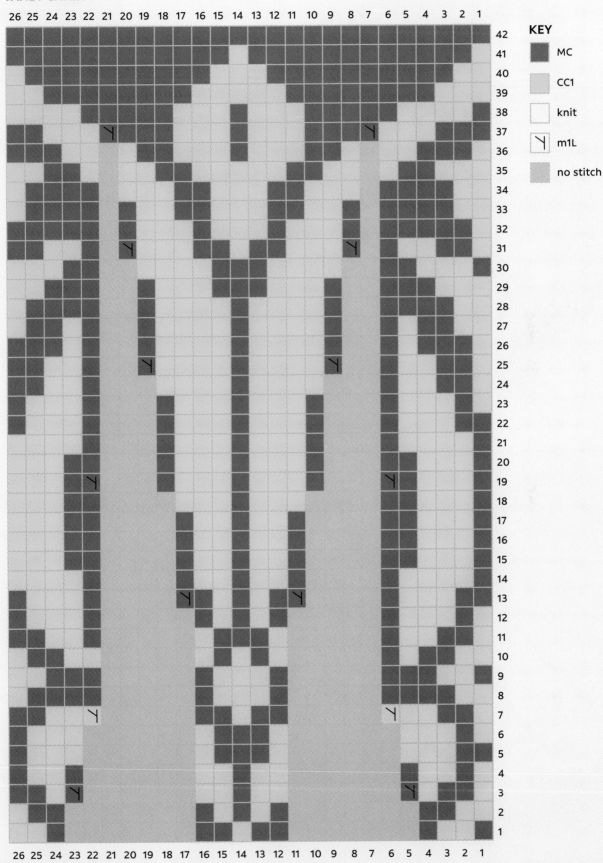

KEY

- ■ MC
- ▨ CC1
- □ knit
- ⅄ m1L
- ▨ no stitch

MILA

Mila was inspired by stained glass windows and how the sun shines through them, with the light playing with shadows and hue. Choose three colors with lots of contrast between each other. You can choose a speckled yarn for a fun effect, but make sure the speckles don't interfere with all of the other colors.

The single ply yarn I used gives the sweater a slight shine, which adds to the stained glass imagery. Look for a fiber with a bit of silk content if you wish to achieve a similar result.

YARN YARDAGE / METERAGE

Yarn: La Bien Aimée Merino Singles, 100% merino, 100g 400 yards / 366 meters

SIZE	1	2	3	4	5	6	7	8	9	10
MC: "ROMANCE"	765	829	892	956	1020	1084	1147	1211	1275	1339 yd
	700	758	816	874	933	991	1049	1107	1166	1224 m
CC1: "ASH"	118	139	160	181	202	223	244	265	286	307 yd
	108	127	146	166	185	204	223	242	262	281 m
CC2: "YELLOW BRICK ROAD"	84	101	120	138	156	174	192	210	228	246 yd
	77	92	110	126	143	159	176	192	208	225 m

PATTERN NOTES

Choose three colors with high contrast. This yoke has several rounds where you'll be knitting three colors at a time. Try holding the two most-used colors in one hand and the third color in the other. Check your tension especially during these rounds to keep the gauge consistent.

MILA CHART

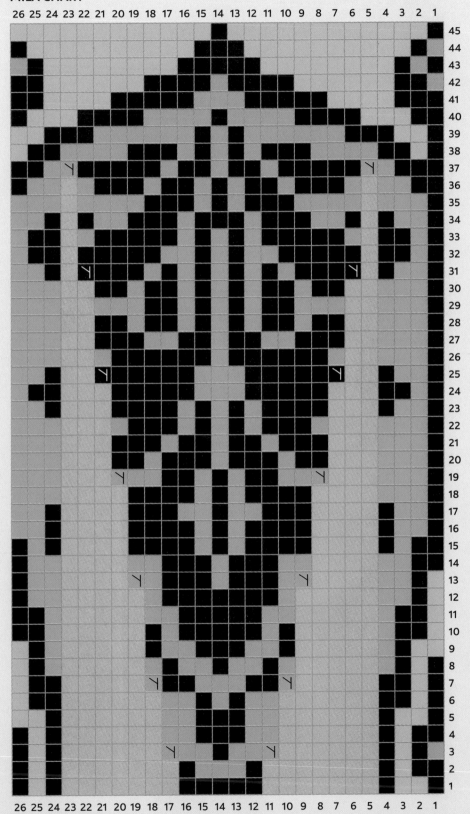

KEY

- ▨ MC
- ■ CC1
- ▨ CC2
- □ knit
- ⅄ m1L
- ▨ no stitch

FINLEY

Finley was inspired by flowers, which I love to grow and often use for inspiration.

You can choose two colors for this design - with lots of contrast for a bold look, or with less contrast for a softer look. Using a variegated colorful yarn for your contrast color would create an interesting effect. Just make sure the main color you use is different from any of the colors in the contrast yarn.

Play around with different options and make sure to make a swatch with the two colors together to see how they play with each other.

YARN YARDAGE / METERAGE

Yarn: Camellia Fiber Co. CFC Sylvan Fingering, 70% alpaca / 20% silk / 10% cashmere, 100g 437 yards / 400 meters

SIZE	1	2	3	4	5	6	7	8	9	10
MC: "CHICORY"	1143	1238	1333	1429	1524	1619	1714	1810	1905	2000 yd
	1045	1132	1219	1307	1394	1481	1567	1655	1742	1829 m
CC1: "PINK AMETHYST"	90	119	138	157	176	195	214	233	252	271 yd
	82	109	126	144	161	178	196	213	230	248 m

PATTERN NOTES

Fingering / 4ply weight sweaters also work great with three-quarter-length sleeves. Knit the sleeves to 2in / 5cm shorter than desired length, then work the cuff ribbing. Skip the last decrease before the cuff, but do make sure the number of stitches is divisible by four to work the 2×2 rib - adjust the stitch count using evenly spaced k2tog decreases around as needed.

FINLEY CHART

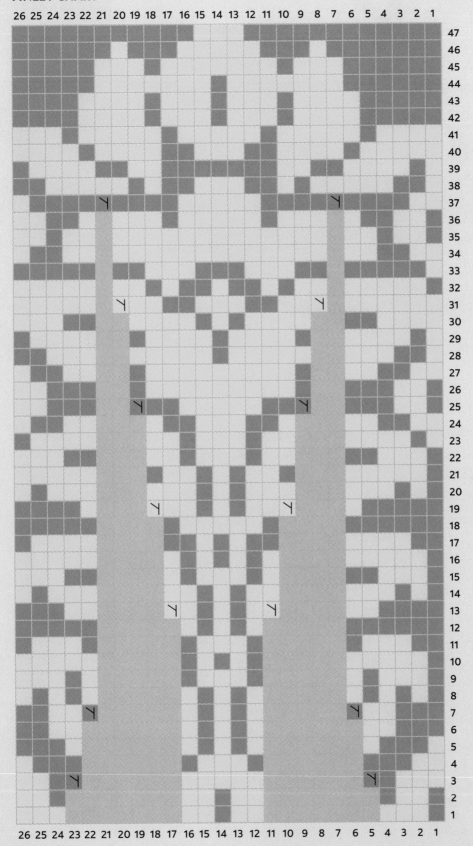

KEY

- ■ MC
- ▨ CC1
- ☐ knit
- ⅄ m1L
- ▒ no stitch

ADELINE

Adeline was worked holding two strands of lace weight yarn together. I loved working with the super soft baby yak base and use this yarn often with my designs. You can also use one strand of fingering / 4ply, light fingering / 3ply or sport / 5ply weight yarn for this sweater if you prefer. Just make sure to swatch and have correct gauge.

A soft yarn with a bit of a halo will create a romantic piece. If you'd like more stitch definition in the motif, use a yarn that's spun tightly.

YARN YARDAGE / METERAGE

Yarn: mYak Baby Yak Lace, 100% baby yak, 50g 370 yards / 339 meters

SIZE	1	2	3	4	5	6	7	8	9	10
MC: "DUSTY PINK"	1893	2039	2184	2330	2476	2621	2767	2912	3058	3204 yd
	1731	1865	1997	2131	2264	2397	2530	2663	2797	2930 m

PATTERN NOTES

Hold the lace weight yarn doubled for this sweater. Maintain a consistent gauge throughout the yoke for a beautiful, even result. Make sure to use the correct type of increase, in knit or purl as indicated in the chart, to maintain the pattern.

The cable stitches use two, three and four stitches, as well as knit and purl stitches, so follow the instructions for each cable symbol carefully. Advanced knitters may want to try working without a cable needle - this technique can take some getting used to, so make sure to practice on your swatch and keep your cabling technique the same for the whole project.

ADELINE CHART

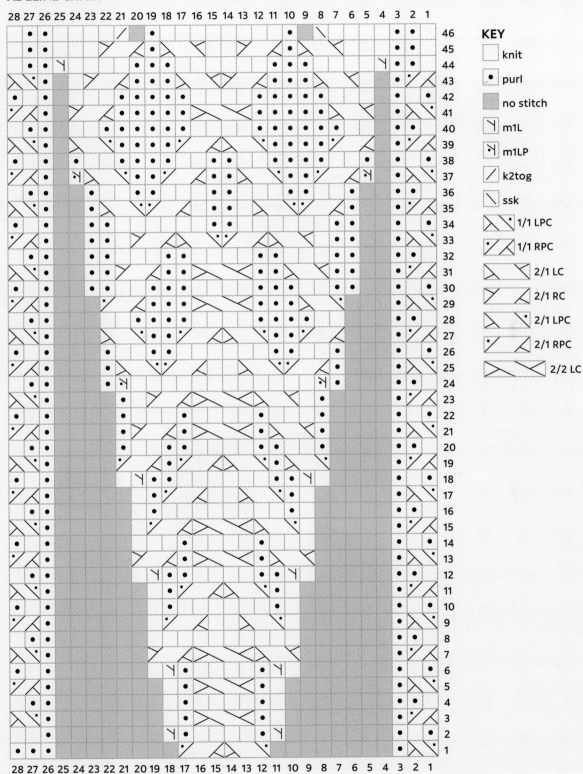

KEY

☐	knit
●	purl
▨	no stitch
⅄	m1L
⅄	m1LP
╱	k2tog
╲	ssk
⟋⟍	1/1 LPC
⟋⟍	1/1 RPC
⟋⟍	2/1 LC
⟋⟍	2/1 RC
⟋⟍	2/1 LPC
⟋⟍	2/1 RPC
⟋⟍	2/2 LC

FINGERING / 4PLY SWEATER PATTERN

Fingering / 4ply weight sweaters are so great in any season! They can be worn on a chilly summer evening or layered in the colder months. The thinner yarn allows for intricate details and, although it takes a bit more time to knit into a sweater, the results are so pleasing.

For the four designs in this chapter, you can use fingering / 4ply, sport / 5ply, or light fingering / 3ply weight with a strand of lace held together, or lace weight held double (as in Adeline sweater). As long as you get the correct gauge and are happy with the fabric the yarn creates with the gauge, then you are ready to start knitting!

PATTERN

Using smaller gauge needles and Janey MC / Mila CC1 / Adeline MC / Finley MC, loosely cast on (96,104,112) 112,116,120 (124,128,132) 132 sts using long tail or your preferred method. PM for back of neck and join to work in the round. This will be your BOR.

R1: *k1, p1* rep to BOR.

Repeat R1 four more times.

Switch to main gauge needles.

Increase round 1: *k2, m1L* to end.

(144,156,168) 168,174,180 (186,192,198) 198 sts

SHORT ROW NECK SHAPING

I suggest using the German short row method, as it is the least visible one, in my opinion. You are welcome to use your favorite short row technique, where the instructions read "turn".

R1 (right side): k (36,40,44) 44,46,48 (50,52,54) 56, turn.

R2 (wrong side): purl back to BOR, sm, p (36,40,44) 44,46,48 (50,52,54) 56, turn.

R3 (right side): knit to 4 sts past the last turned st, turn.

R4 (wrong side): purl to 4 sts past the last turned st, turn.

Repeat R3 and R4 two more times. Knit to BOR.

Knit one round, resolving the turned sts as you come to them (pick up the loop you previously wrapped around a stitch to turn for a short row, and knit it together with said stitch).

INCREASE ROUND 2 (SIZES 4-10 ONLY)

Size 4: *k14, m1L* rep to BOR.

Size 5: *k9, m1L, k10, m1L, k10, m1L* rep to BOR.

Size 6:*k7, m1L, k8, m1L* rep to BOR.

Size 7: *k7, m1L, (k6, m1L) four times* rep to BOR.

Size 8: *k6, m1L, (k5, m1L) two times* rep to BOR.

Size 9: *(k5, m1L) three times, k4, m1L* rep to last 8 sts, (k4, m1L) two times.

Size 10: *(k3, m1L, k4, m1L) two times, (k4, m1L) two times* rep to BOR.

(144,156,168) 180,192,204 (216,228,240) 252 sts

Work chart.

(312,338,364) 390,416,442 (468,494,520) 546 sts

Continue with MC in stockinette / stocking stitch until work measures (8,8.5,9) 9.5,10,10.25 (10.5,10.75,11) 11.25 in / (20.5,21.5,23) 24,25.5,26 (26.5,27.5,28) 28.5 cm from front cast on edge. This is a good time to try on your yoke to make sure it fits your unique size and personal style. If needed, you can add more length before separating for sleeves. Just remember that this will add a bit more yarn than specified in the yardage / meterage requirements.

Remove BOR marker.

K (44,49,53) 58,63,68 (72,76,80) 84 sts.

Place the following (68,71,76) 79,82,85 (90,95,100) 105 sts on scrap yarn, for right sleeve.

Using the backwards loop method, cast on (8,10,14) 16,18,20 (24,28,32) 36 sts.

Knit the following (88,98,106) 116,126,136 (144,152,160) 168 sts.

Place the following (68,71,76) 79,82,85 (90,95,100) 105 sts on scrap yarn, for left sleeve.

Using the backwards loop method, cast on (8,10,14) 16,18,20 (24,28,32) 36 sts, placing a marker in the middle of these sts, for BOR.

(192,216,240) 264,288,312 (336,360,384) 408 sts

Continue in stockinette / stocking stitch st in the round until body measures 11in / 28cm when measured from the cast on underarm sts, or until the body is 2in / 5cm shorter than your total preferred length.

HEM

Switch to smaller gauge needles.

R1: *k2, p2* rep to BOR.

Repeat R1 until hem measures 2in / 5cm.

Bind / cast off loosely, in pattern.

SLEEVES

Both sleeves are worked the same way.

Move one set of (68,71,76) 79,82,85 (90,95,100) 105 sleeve sts onto needles. Starting where the sts end and underarm begins, using MC, pick up and knit (8,10,14) 16,18,20 (24,28,32) 36 sts, plus one stitch on each side in the gap where the sleeve sts meet the underarm sts. PM in the middle of these underarm sts. This will be the BOR.

(78,83,92) 97,102,107 (116,125,134) 143 sts

R1: Knit until 1 st of the sleeve sts remains (before picked up sts), ssk, knit to BOR.

R2: Knit to the last picked up st (before sleeve sts), k2tog, knit to BOR.

(76,81,90) 95,100,105 (114,123,132) 141 sts

SLEEVE DECREASES

Step 1: knit (6,6,6) 5,4,4 (4,3,3) 3 rounds.

Step 2: k3, k2tog, knit to last 5 sts, ssk, k3.

Repeat Steps 1 and 2 (9,7,9) 10,9,11 (13,18,20) 22 more times. (56,65,70) 73,80,81 (86,85,90) 95 sts

Then continue in stockinette / stocking stitch until sleeve measures 15in / 38cm when measured from the cast on underarm sts, or until the sleeve is 2in / 5cm shorter than your total preferred length.

DEC. ROUND

Size 1: *k5, k2tog* rep to BOR.

Sizes 2,3,5,8,9,10: *k3, k2tog* rep to BOR.

Size 4: k5, k2tog, *k4, k2tog* rep to BOR.

Sizes 6,7: k4, k2tog, *k3, k2tog* rep to BOR.

(48,52,56) 61,64,65 (69,68,72) 76 sts

Knit one round.

CUFF

Switch to smaller gauge needles.

Sizes 1,2,3,5,8,9,10: *k2, p2* rep to BOR.

Sizes 4,6,7: k2tog, k1, p2, *k2, p2* rep to BOR.

(--,--,--) 60,--,64 (68,--,--) -- sts

Continue in 2×2 rib until cuff measures 2in / 5cm.

Bind / cast off loosely, in pattern.

Repeat for second sleeve.

FINISHING

When you are done knitting your sweater, you'll need to do some finishing work to ensure lasting and professional looking results.

First you'll need to weave in all the yarn ends poking out where you began and ended sections of the sweater. Use a tapestry needle to weave in the ends loosely on the wrong side of the work, then carefully snip off the remaining yarn.

And last but not least, block your project. Soak your completed sweater in room temperature water and a little bit of wool wash, for 15-20 minutes. Next, pull it out of the water and squeeze it out. If you are using a yarn of animal fibers, you have to be careful here - gently squeeze the knitted fabric and do not agitate it as this risks felting the fabric. I will often lay the sweater between two towels, roll it up and gently walk on the rolled up towels. Now you'll want to lay the sweater out and shape it, to dry. It will dry in whatever form you leave it in, so make sure you shape it to the measurement specifications for your size.

Once your sweater is dry, you can wear it! Enjoy your hard work and stay cozy!

CABLE STITCHES

To make a cable, you will slip a specified number of stitches onto a cable needle and place the cable needle either at the front or the back of your work. The number in the abbreviation indicates how many stitches are placed on the cable needle and how many next stitches are worked. The L or R indicates whether it is a left or right cross, and if there is a P, it indicates that some of the stitches are worked as purl stitches.

The pictures below show cables using four stitches (two held on the cable needle and two worked off the left hand needle).

For the 2/2 LC the next two stitches on the left hand needle are placed on the cable needle and held at the front of the work. The next two stitches are worked from the left hand needle and then the two stitches from the cable needle are worked, creating a left cross.

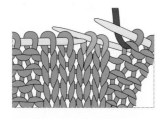 

For the 2/2 RC the next two stitches on the left hand needle are placed on the cable needle and held at the back of the work. The next two stitches are worked from the left hand needle and then the two stitches from the cable needle are worked, creating a right cross.

Other cables are worked in a similar manner, following the instructions as listed for each specific cable abbreviation.

CABLE STITCH ABBREVIATIONS AND INSTRUCTIONS

1/1 LC - 1/1 left cross: place one stitch on a cable needle and hold to front of work; knit the following stitch, then knit the stitch on the cable needle.

1/1 RC - 1/1 right cross: place one stitch on a cable needle and hold to back of work; knit the following stitch, then knit the stitch on the cable needle.

1/1 LPC - 1/1 left purl cross: place one stitch on a cable needle and hold to front of work; purl the following stitch, then knit the stitch on the cable needle.

1/1 RPC - 1/1 right cross: place one stitch on a cable needle and hold to back of work; knit the following stitch, then purl the stitch on the cable needle.

2/1 LC - 2/1 left cross: place two stitches on a cable needle and hold to front of work; knit the following stitch, then knit the stitches on the cable needle.

2/1 RC - 2/1 right cross: place one stitch on a cable needle and hold to back of work; knit the two following stitches, then knit the stitch on the cable needle.

2/1 LPC - 2/1 left purl cross: place two stitches on a cable needle and hold to front of work; purl the following stitch, then knit the stitches on the cable needle.

2/1 RPC - 2/1 right cross: place one stitch on a cable needle and hold to back of work; knit the two following stitches, then purl the stitch on the cable needle.

2/2 LC - 2/2 left cross: place two stitches on a cable needle and hold to front of work; knit the two following stitches, then knit the stitches on the cable needle.

2/2 RC - 2/2 right cross: place two stitches on a cable needle and hold to back of work; knit the two following stitches, then knit the stitches on the cable needle.

2/2 LPC - 2/2 left purl cross: place two stitches on a cable needle and hold to front of work; knit the two following stitches, then purl the stitches on the cable needle.

2/2 RPC - 2/2 right purl cross: place two stitches on a cable needle and hold to back of work; purl the two following stitches, then purl the stitches on the cable needle.

ABBREVIATIONS

The following abbreviations are used in this book:

bobble	make a bobble, in your favorite way; I suggest half double crochet bobbles
BOR	beginning of round
CC1	contrast color 1
CC2	contrast color 2
dec	decrease
inc	increase
k	knit
k2tog	knit two together
MC	main color
m1L	make one left leaning
m1LP	make one left leaning purlwise
m1R	make one right leaning
m1RP	make one right leaning purlwise
p	purl
PM	place marker
R	round / row
rep	repeat
sm	slip marker
ssk	slip, slip, knit these sts together
st(s)	stitch(es)
stockinette / stocking stitch	in the round, work as all knit stitches; when working short rows, knit on right side rows and purl on wrong side rows
1x1 rib	k1, p1 rib
2x2 rib	k2, p2 rib
**	repeat instructions between stars, until specified
( )	repeat within a repeat

BASIC KNITTING SKILLS

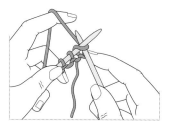 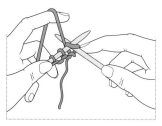  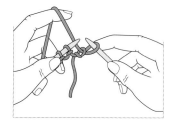

KNIT STITCH (CONTINENTAL STYLE)

Keep the yarn behind the left hand needle. Insert the right hand needle into the next stitch on the left hand needle from front to back of work. Catch the working yarn, moving the needle downwards and pull it through the stitch being knitted. Let the stitch fall off the left hand needle.

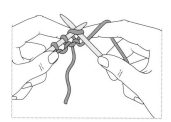  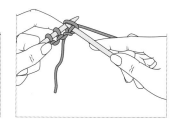 

KNIT STITCH (ENGLISH STYLE)

With yarn at back of the work, insert the right hand needle into the next stitch on the left hand needle from left to right (knitwise). Wrap the working yarn counterclockwise / anticlockwise around the right hand needle tip and pull it through the stitch being knitted. Let the stitch fall off the left hand needle.

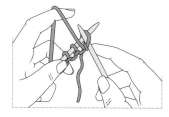 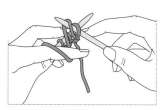  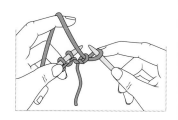

PURL STITCH (CONTINENTAL STYLE)

Keep the yarn in front of the left hand needle. Insert the right hand needle into the next stitch on the left hand needle from back to front of work. Place the yarn over and under the right hand needle, catch it and pull it through the stitch being worked. Let the stitch fall off the left hand needle.

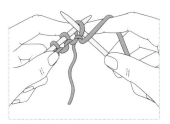  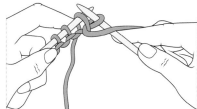 

PURL STITCH (ENGLISH STYLE)

With the yarn at the front of the work, insert the right hand needle into the next stitch on the left hand needle from right to left (purlwise). Wrap the working yarn counterclockwise / anticlockwise around the right hand needle tip and pull it through the stitch being knitted. Let the stitch fall off the left hand needle.

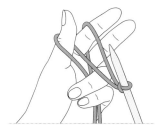 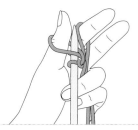  

LONG TAIL CAST ON

Make a slipknot, leaving a very long tail (about 3 yards / 3 meters). Hold the slipknot on a knitting needle in your right hand. Place your left index finger and thumb downward into the space between the two yarn strands, with the tail closer to your thumb. Now, flip your left hand up, causing the yarn to go around your finger and thumb, and end up in the inside of your finger and thumb and holding the yarn with tension. *Insert the needle from the bottom into the loop on your thumb, and into the loop on your index finger from the top, and pull it through the loop on your thumb. Let the yarn slide off your thumb and lightly tighten up the stitch on the needle. Now place your thumb back between the two yarn strands and flip it up to its original position. Repeat from * until you have the desired amount of stitches.

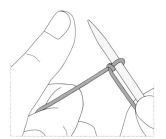 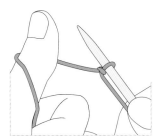  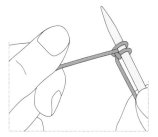

BACKWARDS LOOP CAST ON

Place your left thumb over the yarn as close to where it is attached to the last stitch as possible. While holding the yarn with your other fingers, move your thumb away from you, over and under the yarn – creating a loop around your thumb. Insert the right hand needle from the bottom up through the loop on your thumb. Tighten up the stitch until it's next to the last worked stitch. Repeat for each stitch to cast on.

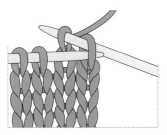 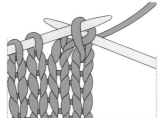 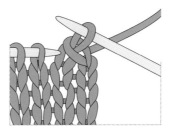 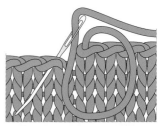

BIND / CAST OFF

Knit two stitches. Insert the left hand needle into the first worked stitch and pull it over the second stitch and let it fall off the needle. There is now one stitch on the right hand needle. *Knit one, pull the first stitch over the stitch you just knitted and let it go. Continue from * until one stitch remains on the right hand needle. Cut the yarn and pull the tail through the last stitch and tighten. Use the tapestry needle to pull the yarn through the first bound off stitch of the round and fasten off.

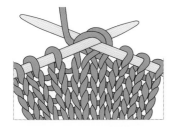

K2TOG

Insert right hand needle knit wise into the second and then first st on the left hand needle, knit both stitches together.

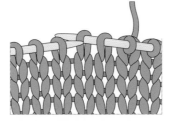 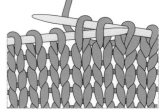

SSK

With right hand needle, slip first stitch off left hand needle knit wise, then the second one, too. Place both stitches back onto left hand needle at the same time, purl wise, and knit these two stitches together through the back loop.

MAKE 1 LEFT LEANING (M1L)

With left hand needle, pick up the strand of yarn that connects the two stitches you are between, from front to back. Insert right hand needle into this loop, as if to knit through the back loop (back to front), and knit.

MAKE 1 LEFT LEANING PURLWISE (M1LP)

With left hand needle, pick up the strand of yarn that connects the two stitches you are between, from front to back. With yarn in front, insert the right hand needle from back to front through the back of the stitch, and purl it.

Make 1 left leaning

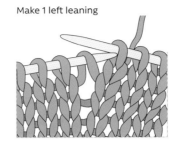 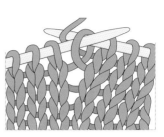

MAKE 1 RIGHT LEANING (M1R)

With left hand needle, pick up the strand of yarn that connects the two stitches you are between, from back to front. Insert right hand needle into this loop as if to knit (front to back), and knit.

MAKE 1 RIGHT LEANING PURLWISE (M1RP)

With left hand needle, pick up the strand of yarn that connects the two stitches you are between, from back to front. With yarn in front, insert the right hand needle from back to front and purl.

Make 1 right leaning

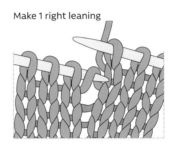 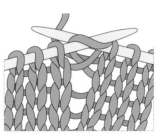

OTHER TECHNIQUES

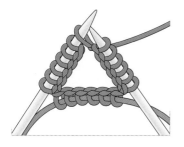 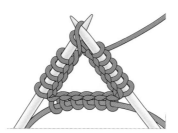 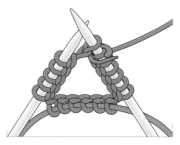

JOIN IN THE ROUND

The least noticeable way to join in the round, and which I recommend most: after casting on specified number of stitches, cast on one more. Make sure your stitches aren't twisted anywhere on your needles and bring the two ends together. Slip the extra stitch you cast on from the right hand needle to the left hand needle. Bring the first stitch on your left hand needle over this extra stitch. Place the marker on the right hand needle and slip the extra stitch back onto the right hand needle. This stitch now has an appearance of a knitted stitch, so treat it as your first worked stitch in this first round.

Turn after a right side row 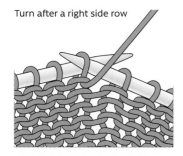 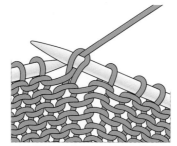 Turn after a wrong side row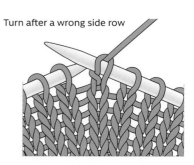

GERMAN SHORT ROWS

Turn after a right side row: Work as instructed until specified. Turn work to wrong side and place the working yarn under and to the back of needle (to the right side of work). Place the first stitch onto right hand needle. Pull the yarn over the top of needle and towards you, holding tight. The turn is complete. Continue by working the following stitches, as instructed in the pattern.

Turn after a wrong side row: Work as instructed until specified. Turn work to right side and place the working yarn under and to the front of needle. Place the first stitch onto right hand needle. Pull the yarn over the top of needle and away from you. holding tight. The turn is complete. Continue by working the following stitches, as instructed in the pattern.

  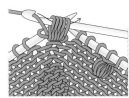  

HALF DOUBLE CROCHET BOBBLE

Insert a crochet hook into the stitch knitwise from front to back and pull up a loop from the working yarn leaving the stitch on the left hand needle. Work a yarn over. Pull up another loop in the same way. Work another yarn over, and pull up one more loop, all the while not letting the stitch off the left hand needle (five stitches on hook). Catch the working yarn with your hook and pull it through all five stitches (one stitch on hook). Catch the yarn again and pull through the loop on your hook, insert the hook knitwise into the original stitch on your left hand needle, and pull up another stitch, letting the stitch fall from the left hand needle (two stitches on hook). Catch the yarn one more time and pull through these two stitches (one stitch on hook). Place the remaining stitch on your hook onto the right hand needle and continue to the next stitch, as instructed.

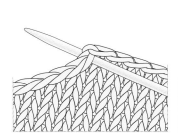 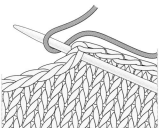 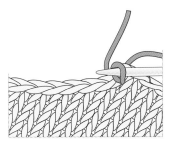 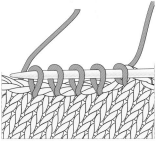

PICKING UP STITCHES

Insert the needle into the stitch or space between stitches from front to back of the work. Wrap the yarn around the needle as if you were working a knit stitch, and pull the loop on the needle through to the front of the work to create a new stitch. Continue in the same way, evenly creating new stitches as instructed until you have the required number of stitches.

PHOTO CREDIT: Kristen Rice Photography

ABOUT THE AUTHOR

Olga Putano is a Ukrainian knitwear designer who now resides on a farm in the Northeastern US with her husband and their four children.

She consistently designs colorwork sweaters, but enjoys learning and utilizing different and new-to-her knitting techniques. Her patterns are designed to encourage knitters to add beautiful knitwear to their handmade closet.

Aside from knitting, Olga loves spending time outdoors with her family, sewing, gardening, and growing her sustainable family farm.

Ravelry: OlgaPutanoDesigns
Instagram: @olgaputanodesigns
Website: olgaputanodesigns.com

ACKNOWLEDGEMENTS

When I started designing knitting patterns in 2018, I had this dream of one day writing a book. Being brand new in a world of many talented designers, it was certainly an ambitious dream. I will always remember and be grateful for Sarah at David and Charles for reaching out to me with the idea of this book. Yoke sweaters is something I consistently design and enjoy creating, so it felt very natural (while also exhilarating) to agree to the project. Thank you to each person at David and Charles who worked with me on this book. Your kindness and patience were evident in each conversation.

I dedicate this book to God, who gifted me the skills and allowed me to realize this dream; and to my mother, who taught me how to knit. A special thank you to my husband, for being so very supportive in the excitement as well as the trials of working on this big project. To my sister Nadya, who repeatedly and selflessly took all four of our children on exciting adventures and for gifting me several hours of silence each time, to work on this book. Thank you also to my family and few friends who asked and listened to me lovingly as I went through all of the emotions that come with working hard on achieving this dream.

INDEX

A DAVID AND CHARLES BOOK
© David and Charles, Ltd 2023

David and Charles is an imprint of David and Charles, Ltd
Suite A, Tourism House, Pynes Hill, Exeter, EX2 5WS

Text and Designs © Olga Putano 2023
Layout and Photography © David and Charles, Ltd 2023

First published in the UK and USA in 2023

A catalogue record for this book is available from the British Library.

ISBN-13: 9781446309469 paperback
ISBN-13: 9781446382028 EPUB
ISBN-13: 9781446382011 PDF

This book has been printed on paper from approved suppliers and made from pulp from sustainable sources.

Printed in Turkey by Omur for:
David and Charles, Ltd
Suite A, Tourism House, Pynes Hill, Exeter, EX2 5WS

10 9 8 7 6 5 4 3 2 1

Publishing Director: Ame Verso
Senior Commissioning Editor: Sarah Callard
Managing Editor: Jeni Chown
Editor: Jessica Cropper
Project Editor: Tricia Gilbert
Head of Design: Anna Wade
Design and Art Direction: Sarah Rowntree
Pre-press Designer: Ali Stark
Illustrations: Kuo Kang Chen
Photography: Jason Jenkins
Production Manager: Beverley Richardson

David and Charles publishes high-quality books on a wide range of subjects. For more information visit www.davidandcharles.com.

Share your makes with us on social media using #dandcbooks and follow us on Facebook and Instagram by searching for @dandcbooks.

Layout of the digital edition of this book may vary depending on reader hardware and display settings.